Exploring Food Chains and Food Webs

BACKYARD
FOOD CHAINS

Katie Kawa

PowerKiDS
press.

New York

Published in 2015 by The Rosen Publishing Group, Inc.
29 East 21st Street, New York, NY 10010

Copyright © 2015 by The Rosen Publishing Group, Inc.

All rights reserved. No part of this book may be reproduced in any form without permission in writing from the publisher, except by a reviewer.

First Edition

Editor: Katie Kawa
Book Design: Reann Nye

Photo Credits: Cover Stan Osolinski/Oxford Scientific/Getty Images; p. 5 (backyard) Jamie Hooper/Shutterstock.com; pp. 5, 21 (strawberries) sevenke/Shutterstock.com; pp. 5, 21 (slug) Lisa S./Shutterstock.com; pp. 5, 21 (robin) Nancy Bauer/Shutterstock.com; pp. 5, 21 (cat) HHelene/Shutterstock.com; p. 7 Velychko/Shutterstock.com; p. 8 MBoe/Shutterstock.com; p. 9 Gary C. Tognoni/Shutterstock.com; p. 10 Hinterhaus Productions/Digital Vision/Getty Images; p. 11 Nadieshda/Moment Open/Getty Images; pp. 12, 21 (caterpillar) Ron Rowan Photography/Shutterstock.com; p. 13 Cavan Images/Photonica/Getty Images; p. 14 Cameron Watson/Shutterstock.com; p. 15 (praying mantis) Alexander Ishchenko/Shutterstock.com; p. 15 (owl) Mark Medcalf/Shutterstock.com; p. 17 Gerald A. DeBoer/Shutterstock.com; pp. 18, 21 (bacteria) Zhukov/Shutterstock.com; pp. 19, 21 (mushrooms) Nikita Rogul/Shutterstock.com; p. 21 (person) Felix Mizioznikov/Shutterstock.com; p. 21 (owl) Philip Ellard/Shutterstock.com; p. 21 (mouse) CreativeNature.nl/Shutterstock.com; p. 21 (lettuce) Humannet/Shutterstock.com; p. 21 (rabbit) Leena Robinson/Shutterstock.com; p. 21 (raccoon) jadimages/Shutterstock.com; p. 21 (carrots) Denis and Yulia Pogostins/Shutterstock.com; p. 21 (grass) Smileus/Shutterstock.com; p. 21 (backyard) Nanisimova/Shutterstock.com; p. 22 cleanfotos/Shutterstock.com.

Library of Congress Cataloging-in-Publication Data

Kawa, Katie. author.
 Backyard food chains / Katie Kawa.
     pages cm. — (Exploring food chains and food webs)
 Includes index.
 ISBN 978-1-4994-0050-2 (pbk.)
 ISBN 978-1-4994-0051-9 (6 pack)
 ISBN 978-1-4994-0045-8 (library binding)
 1. Food chains (Ecology)—Juvenile literature. 2. Urban ecology (Biology)—Juvenile literature. 3. Nature—Effect of human beings on—Juvenile literature. I. Title.
 QH541.15.F66K39 2015
 577.5'6—dc23
                                          2014032897

Manufactured in the United States of America

CPSIA Compliance Information: Batch #CW15PK: For Further Information contact Rosen Publishing, New York, New York at 1-800-237-9932

CONTENTS

NEARBY FOOD CHAINS

Food chains show how plants and animals in an **ecosystem** are connected by what they eat and what eats them. They show the ways **energy** is passed from one living thing to another. A group of food chains connected together is called a food web.

Where can you find food chains in action? One of the easiest places to see food chains is your own backyard! If you don't have a backyard, you can see food chains in action at a park or playground. Look carefully, because some members of these backyard food chains are very small.

Food Chain Fact

The sun is an important part of food chains. It gives plants the energy that's passed on to the animals that eat them.

STRAWBERRIES

SLUG

CAT

ROBIN

This food chain shows the connections between plants and animals in a backyard. The arrows represent, or stand for, the flow of energy from one living thing to another.

BACKYARD HABITATS

Every living thing needs a place where it can find food, water, and somewhere to live. This is a habitat. Backyards are a special kind of habitat filled with plants and animals that are very familiar to people.

People live in their own habitats, and backyards can be part of those habitats. People might grow food in their backyard. They could also use a backyard to play, work, and even cook. People leave their mark on backyard habitats in many ways, including planting things that other animals use for food, such as flowers.

Food Chain Fact

People **introduce** animals into backyard habitats when they get pets, such as dogs and cats.

A vegetable garden is an example of people getting food from a backyard habitat.

STARTING WITH THE SUN

The sun is the starting point for all food chains, including those in your backyard. It's where all the energy in a food chain originally comes from.

Lettuce is a common plant grown in backyard gardens. It gets its energy directly from the sun. It uses much of this energy to live and grow, but the leftover energy is stored in the plant. Rabbits like to eat the lettuce that grows in backyards. When a rabbit eats lettuce, the sun's energy that was stored in the plant is passed on to the rabbit.

Food Chain Fact

Rabbits and other animals store energy in their body, which gets passed on to the animals that eat them.

When a barn owl eats a rabbit, it's still getting some energy from the sun because of the way energy is passed from the sun to the lettuce, to the rabbit, and, finally, to the owl.

PRODUCERS AND CONSUMERS

Plants turn sunlight, water, and **carbon dioxide** into energy that can be used by living things. They do this through a **process** called photosynthesis (foh-toh-SIHN-thuh-suhs), which creates a kind of sugar plants use for food. A backyard garden is filled with examples of plants using energy from the sun to grow. Flowers, trees, and vegetables live and grow because of the food they make through photosynthesis.

Plants are called producers because they produce their own food from the sun's energy. Animals are called consumers because they consume, or eat, plants and other animals.

Food Chain Fact

Photosynthesis also produces oxygen, which is a gas animals need to live.

Carrots are producers because they make their own food through photosynthesis. People are consumers because they eat carrots and other plants.

HELPFUL HERBIVORES

Producers are just the first **link** in a backyard food chain. Animals that eat them are the next link. People aren't the only ones who eat the plants that grow in a backyard. Squirrels and caterpillars are just two of the many animals that get their energy from plants. These plant-eating animals are called herbivores.

Sometimes plants need herbivores, too. When a squirrel finishes eating an apple that fell from a tree, it could carry a seed from that apple to another backyard. The seed will grow into a new apple tree.

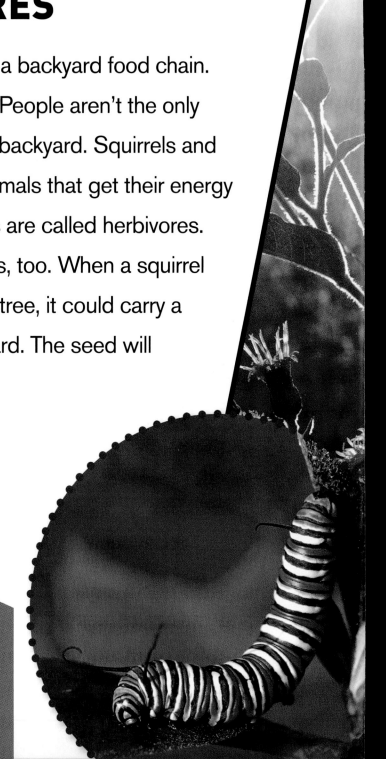

Food Chain Fact

Caterpillars eat leaves and grass. When they grow into butterflies, they eat the nectar of flowers.

Butterflies and flowers help each other survive. Flowers give butterflies nectar to eat. Butterflies carry pollen from one flower to another. This allows flowers to reproduce, or make new flowers.

THE HUNTERS AND THE HUNTED

Backyards may not look like scary places, but they're very scary for some animals. This is because backyards are home to many carnivores, or animals that eat other animals. Predators live in backyards, looking for the animals they hunt for food. The animals that are hunted are called prey.

All three of these backyard creatures are carnivores. Cats and barn owls hunt many of the same animals, including mice and rabbits.

Birds are common backyard predators that kill and eat bugs. Robins like to eat caterpillars. Robins can then be eaten by cats. Cats that eat robins are called secondary carnivores because they eat other carnivores. Cats also eat mice, and they sometimes eat rabbits, too.

Food Chain Fact

Some insects are also carnivores. The praying mantis eats other insects, including other praying mantises!

EATING IT ALL!

Some backyard animals eat both plants and other animals. They're called omnivores. Many omnivores will eat anything they can find, including people's garbage. Raccoons are common backyard omnivores. They eat out of people's trash cans, but they also eat nuts, berries, bugs, eggs, mice, seeds, and many other things.

Crows are also omnivores. These birds will even eat the bodies of dead animals they find. Animals that find and eat dead animals are called scavengers. Scavengers are important because they make sure no energy left in an animal's body goes to waste.

Food Chain Fact

The parts of dead animals and plants left behind in the soil are broken down by creatures called decomposers.

Raccoons are nocturnal, which means they're most active at night.

A DIRTY JOB

Decomposers are a very important part of all food chains, including ones found in backyards. When they break down the bodies of dead plants and animals, they put **nutrients** back into the soil. Plants use their roots to get nutrients from the soil. Without decomposers, plants wouldn't have enough nutrients to live. Without plants, nothing else in a backyard could live!

Most backyard decomposers are creatures too small to be seen with human eyes. They're called bacteria. Billions of bacteria can live in just one backyard. Mushrooms are also common backyard decomposers.

Food Chain Fact

Most bacteria can only be seen through a **microscope**.

18

Mushrooms and bacteria break down dead plant and animal matter. Their job is to make the soil rich and full of nutrients so plants can grow.

A BACKYARD FOOD WEB

Food webs show how all the living things in a habitat are connected. The many food chains in a backyard habitat come together to make one backyard food web.

The colors used to outline the living things in this food web show the many kinds of creatures you can find in a backyard habitat. Follow the arrows to trace the flow of energy from one living thing to another. The decomposers are shown in the top right corner of the food web. When all the living things in this web die, their bodies are broken down by the decomposers.

Food Chain Fact

Other foods commonly grown in backyards include tomatoes, beans, and peppers.

Food Web Key

- carnivore
- decomposer
- herbivore
- omnivore
- producer

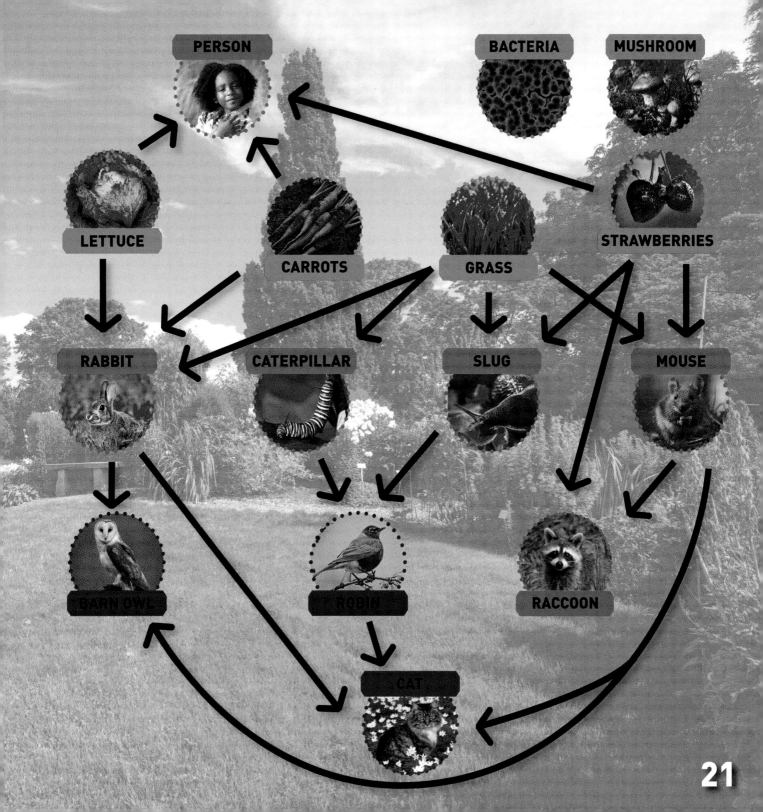

SEE FOR YOURSELF

It's fun to see food chains in action in your own backyard, neighborhood park, or school playground. One good way to learn about backyard food chains is to plant something. Look closely when you dig in the soil. You'll see many creatures living there, including worms.

The more time you spend in a backyard habitat, the more you'll learn about the food chains that are formed there. In the morning, you might see rabbits eating grass or a cat hunting mice. At night, you might see raccoons looking for food. There's so much to see right in your own backyard!

GLOSSARY

carbon dioxide: A gas that's taken in by plants as part of photosynthesis and put back into the air when animals breathe.

ecosystem: A community of living things.

energy: The power or ability to be active.

introduce: To bring in.

link: A connecting piece.

microscope: A tool that makes small objects appear larger when a person looks through it.

nutrient: Something taken in by a plant or animal that helps it grow and stay healthy.

process: A series of actions or changes.

INDEX

B
bacteria, 18, 19, 21

C
carnivores, 14, 15, 20
consumers, 10, 11

D
decomposers, 16, 18, 20

E
ecosystem, 4
energy, 4, 5, 8, 9, 10, 12, 16, 20

G
gardens, 7, 8, 10

H
habitat, 6, 7, 20, 22
herbivores, 12, 20

M
mushrooms, 18, 19, 21

N
nutrients, 18, 19

O
omnivores, 16, 20

P
people, 6, 7, 11, 12, 21
photosynthesis, 10, 11
predators, 14, 15
prey, 14
producers, 10, 11, 12, 20

S
scavengers, 16
secondary carnivores, 15
sun, 4, 8, 9, 10

WEBSITES

Due to the changing nature of Internet links, PowerKids Press has developed an online list of websites related to the subject of this book. This site is updated regularly. Please use this link to access the list: www.powerkidslinks.com/fcfw/bfc

J 577.16 KAWA

Kawa, Katie.
Backyard food chains

SOF

R4002688896

SOUTH FULTON BRANCH
Atlanta-Fulton Public Library